11/13

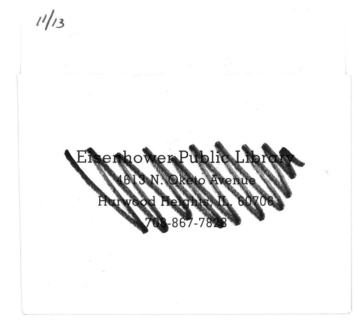

ANIMAL ATTACK!

Hunting with BALD EAGLES

By Paige Thurnherr

Gareth Stevens
Publishing

Please visit our website, www.garethstevens.com. For a free color catalog of all our high-quality books, call toll free 1-800-542-2595 or fax 1-877-542-2596.

Library of Congress Cataloging-in-Publication Data

Thurnherr, Paige.
Hunting with bald eagles / Paige Thurnherr.
    p. cm. — (Animal attack!)
Includes index.
ISBN 978-1-4339-7064-1 (pbk.)
ISBN 978-1-4339-7065-8 (6-pack)
ISBN 978-1-4339-7063-4 (library binding)
1. Bald eagle—Juvenile literature. I. Title.
QL696.F32T49 2012
598.9'43—dc23

                                2011043883

First Edition

Published in 2013 by
Gareth Stevens Publishing
111 East 14th Street, Suite 349
New York, NY 10003

Copyright © 2013 Gareth Stevens Publishing

Designer: Katelyn E. Reynolds
Editor: Greg Roza

Photo credits: Cover, pp. 1, (cover, pp. 1, 3–24 background image) TNWA Photography/Flickr/Getty Images; cover, pp. 1, 3–24 (background graphic) pashabo/Shutterstock.com; cover, pp. 4–23 (splatter graphic) jgl247/Shutterstock.com; p. 5 Paul E. Tessier/Photodisc/Getty Images; pp. 6, 11 FloridaStock/Shutterstock.com; p. 7 Georgescu Gabriel/Shutterstock.com; pp. 9, 12–13 visceralimage/Shutterstock.com; pp. 10, 21 Uryadnikov Sergey/Shutterstock.com; p. 14 Eric Gevaert/Shutterstock.com; p. 15 Lynn Koenig/Flickr/Getty Images; p. 17 Dagny Willis/Flickr/Getty Images; p. 18 Jeff Banke/Shutterstock.com; p. 19 Takayuki Maekawa/The Image Bank/Getty Images; p. 20 Steve Collender/Shutterstock.com.

Printed in the United States of America

CPSIA compliance information: Batch #CS12GS: For further information contact Gareth Stevens, New York, New York at 1-800-542-2595.

CONTENTS

Words in the glossary appear in **bold** type
the first time they are used in the text.

BIRD OF PREY

The bald eagle is a North American raptor. A raptor is a bird of **prey**, or a bird that hunts for and feeds on animals. Bald eagles are very good at hunting fish. In fact, they're sometimes called fishing eagles.

Fish might be the bald eagle's favorite meal, but that's not all it eats. This raptor also eats other birds, squirrels, rabbits, and young deer. They often steal food from other birds. Bald eagles also eat carrion, or dead animals.

Fact Hunter

The Founding Fathers chose the bald eagle as the **emblem** of the United States because of its strength, beauty, and long life.

A bald eagle might make a high-pitched scream
to warn other eagles to stay away.
▼

ARE THEY REALLY BALD?

The bald eagle isn't bald. It has short, snow-white feathers on its head. It also has white feathers on its neck and tail. An adult bald eagle has brownish-black feathers on its back and chest. Its beak and feet are yellow.

Male bald eagles can grow to about 34 inches (86 cm) tall and can have a 7-foot (2.1 m) **wingspan**. Female bald eagles are slightly larger. They can have a 7.5-foot (2.3 m) wingspan.

Fact Hunter

The term "bald" might come from the Old English word for "white": balde.

The bald eagle's size is perfect for hunting and capturing smaller animals.

7

EAGLES EVERYWHERE!

Bald eagles live throughout the United States. They also live everywhere in Canada, except its most northern parts. Many live in Alaska. Some bald eagles **migrate** south in colder months. Some go as far south as northwest Mexico.

Since bald eagles prefer to eat fish, they usually live near water. Many live along the coasts of North America and around the Great Lakes. Others live near major rivers, such as the Missouri and the Mississippi Rivers.

Fact Hunter
Young eagles migrate before their parents do. Scientists aren't sure how they know where to go.

Bald eagles migrate south when northern lakes and rivers freeze over in winter. Many fly to the coasts, where they can still catch fish.

▼

9

HUNTING GROUNDS

A bald eagle's hunting ground can be up to 10,000 acres. This can be much smaller when prey is plentiful. Bald eagles may **perch** on a tall tree or cliff and watch for prey. Or, they **soar** high up, where they have a good view of the land or water below.

Although they're hunters, bald eagles are also **scavengers**. They'll eat larger animals that are already dead, such as seals and deer.

Bald eagles sometimes hunt in pairs or groups.

SOARING AND DIVING

Bald eagles have light bones. They also have broad wings. This allows them to soar for a long time. Bald eagles also use rising currents of warm air—called thermals—to stay in the air even longer when hunting and migrating.

A bald eagle spreads its tail feathers to help catch thermals. The tail works as a brake when landing. It also helps the eagle keep its balance when diving toward the water to catch a fish.

Fact Hunter

If a bald eagle loses a feather on one wing, a feather on the other wing drops off, too. This helps the bird keep its balance.

Bald eagles can reach heights of 10,000 feet (3,048 m). They can reach a speed of 100 miles (161 km) per hour when diving.

▼

13

EAGLE EYES

A bald eagle's vision is four to seven times better than a person's vision. They can't move their eyes, so they need to turn their head to look around. However, a bald eagle's eyes can see both forward and to the side at the same time.

A bald eagle can see a fish beneath the water while soaring several hundred feet above it. From a cliff or branch, it can see small animals on land 1,000 feet (305 m) away!

Bald eagles have two sets of eyelids. One set is for blinking. The other set closes while they sleep.

Bald eagles see in color.

15

TALONS AND BEAKS

Excellent flying skills and eyesight help bald eagles find prey. However, it's the raptor's sharp **talons** and beak that make it such a **fierce** hunter. The bald eagle uses its talons to attack prey. The talons break through the animal's skin and kill it. The bald eagle grabs its meal tightly as it flies back to its nest or perch.

The bald eagle's hooked beak is very strong. The bird uses it to tear and cut food into smaller pieces.

Fact Humor

Bald eagles weigh about 10 pounds (4.5 kg). Their powerful wings and sharp talons allow them to lift about 4 pounds (1.8 kg).

A bald eagle's talons and beak grow
all the time, just like your fingernails.

▼

17

THE HARD LIFE OF AN EAGLET

Both mother and father bald eagles care for their chicks—or eaglets. One guards the eaglets while the other hunts. Adults tear off pieces of prey and feed them to their young.

Adults don't teach their eaglets how to hunt. The chicks must learn by watching adults. Few bald eagle chicks live to adulthood. Some **starve** when food is low. Some die while learning to fly. Others are killed by older, larger chicks while fighting for food.

Bald eagles build some of the biggest nests in the world. They are often 7 feet (2.1 m) across.

TOP OF THE FOOD CHAIN

Bald eagles hunt for many kinds of animals, but they don't have any natural enemies. It probably sounds good to be a bald eagle. However, bald eagles came close to dying out because of the actions of people. Many people hunted eagles. Other eagles died when they flew into power lines and airplanes.

Thanks to a law passed in 1940, bald eagle populations have increased greatly. Many people still work hard to keep these beautiful raptors safe.

Bald Eagle Facts

- In the wild, bald eagles can live about 30 years.

- The oldest **captive** bald eagle lived 48 years.

- It takes about 5 years for young bald eagles to grow white feathers on their head, neck, and tail.

- Bald eagle bones are light because they're hollow.

- Male and female bald eagle couples—called pairs—stay together for life.

- Female bald eagles lay between 1 and 3 eggs every year.

- A group of soaring bald eagles is called a "kettle."

- Bald eagles live in every state except Hawaii.

GLOSSARY

captive: cared for by people, instead of living in the wild

emblem: a picture that stands for a group or country

fierce: likely to attack

migrate: to move from one place to another when the seasons change

perch: to sit or rest on something. Also, the object on which a bird sits or rests.

prey: an animal hunted by other animals for food

scavenger: an animal that eats dead animals or steals food from other animals

soar: to fly high up in the air with little effort

starve: to die from a lack of food

talon: a claw on the foot of a raptor

wingspan: the length from wing tip to wing tip when a bird's wings are stretched out

FOR MORE INFORMATION

Books

Hicks, Kelli L. *The Bald Eagle*. Vero Beach, FL: Rourke Publishing, 2009.

Landau, Elaine. *The Bald Eagle*. New York, NY: Children's Press, 2008.

Magby, Meryl. *Bald Eagles*. New York, NY: PowerKids Press, 2012.

Websites

Bald Eagle
animals.nationalgeographic.com/animals/birds/bald-eagle/
Read more about bald eagles and see pictures of them in the wild.

Birds: Bald Eagle
www.sandiegozoo.org/animalbytes/t-bald_eagle.html
Learn even more about bald eagles from the San Diego Zoo website.

INDEX